Concrete Mixers

Dash!
LEVELED READERS
2

An Imprint of Abdo Zoom • abdobooks.com

2

Dash!
LEVELED READERS

Level 1 – Beginning
Short and simple sentences with familiar words or patterns for children who are beginning to understand how letters and sounds go together.

Level 2 – Emerging
Longer words and sentences with more complex language patterns for readers who are practicing common words and letter sounds.

Level 3 – Transitional
More developed language and vocabulary for readers who are becoming more independent.

abdobooks.com

Published by Abdo Zoom, a division of ABDO, PO Box 398166, Minneapolis, Minnesota 55439.

Printed in the United States of America, North Mankato, Minnesota.
092018
012019

Photo Credits: iStock, Shutterstock
Production Contributors: Kenny Abdo, Jennie Forsberg, Grace Hansen, John Hansen
Design Contributors: Dorothy Toth, Neil Klinepier

Library of Congress Control Number: 2018945598

Publisher's Cataloging in Publication Data

Names: Murray, Julie, author.
Title: Concrete mixers / by Julie Murray.
Description: Minneapolis, Minnesota : Abdo Zoom, 2019 | Series: Construction machines | Includes online resources and index.
Identifiers: ISBN 9781532125140 (lib. bdg.) | ISBN 9781641856591 (pbk) | ISBN 9781532126161 (ebook) | ISBN 9781532126673 (Read-to-me ebook)
Subjects: LCSH: Concrete mixers--Juvenile literature. | Construction equipment--Juvenile literature. | Machinery--Construction--Juvenile literature. | Cement mixers--Juvenile literature.
Classification: DDC 629.225--dc23

THIS BOOK CONTAINS RECYCLED MATERIALS

Table of Contents

Concrete Mixers

Concrete mixers are big trucks. They mix, carry, and pour concrete.

They are used to help build many things, like roads, buildings, and more!

A **concrete** mixer has many parts. It has a cab where the driver sits. It has a water tank and a drum. It also has a **hopper** and **chute**.

10
พี-มิกซ์ คอนกรีต
081-4730075
THAILAND
83-1005

How They Work

Dry **cement** is poured into the **hopper**. Small pieces of gravel are also added. Then, water is added from the tank. It all goes into the drum.

The drum begins to spin. Blades inside the drum mix all the ingredients together. This keeps the **concrete** from hardening.

13

To pour the **concrete**, the blades switch directions. The wet mixture comes out of the **chute**.

A worker guides the **chute**. The wet **concrete** is thick and heavy.

Workers use tools to smooth the **concrete**. They work fast. The concrete dries quickly!

When the job is done, the **concrete** mixer is cleaned. Workers spray water to clean the drum and **chute**.

More Facts

- America's first **concrete** road was built in 1891. It is in Ohio. It is still there today!

- The Ancient Romans made concrete. They mixed water, lime, and volcanic ash.

- Over ten billion tons of concrete is made each year. That is a lot of concrete!

Glossary

cement – a powder made of clay and limestone that becomes hard when water is added.

chute – a long, hallow passage that guides concrete from the truck directly to the job site.

concrete – a hard, strong building material made by mixing sand, gravel, cement, and water.

hopper – a funnel-shaped device used to move concrete into the drum or from the drum into the chute.

Index

Online Resources

Booklinks
NONFICTION NETWORK
FREE! ONLINE NONFICTION RESOURCES

To learn more about concrete mixers, please visit **abdobooklinks.com**. These links are routinely monitored and updated to provide the most current information available.